The Believer's Praise Book

Titles in this series:
> *The Believer's Praise Book*
> *The Believer's Prayer Book*
> *The Believer's Promise Book*
> *The Christian Man's Promise Book*
> *The Christian Woman's Promise Book*
> *Promises From Proverbs*

The Believer's Praise Book

Compiled by LARRY RICHARDS

Zondervan Publishing House
Grand Rapids, Michigan

Daybreak Books are published by Zondervan Publishing House, 1415 Lake Drive, S.E., Grand Rapids, Michigan 49506.

The Believer's Praise Book
Copyright © 1984
by the Zondervan Corporation

Library of Congress Cataloging in Publication Data

Bible. English. New International. Selections. 1984.
  The believer's praise book.

  Praise of God—Biblical teaching. I. Richards, Larry, 1931– . II. Title.
BS195.N37   1984   220.5'2   84-15348
ISBN 0-310-43512-9

Scripture taken from the HOLY BIBLE: NEW INTERNATIONAL VERSION (North American Edition). Copyright © 1973, 1978, 1984 by the International Bible Society. Used by permission of Zondervan Bible Publishers.

All rights reserved. No part of this publication may be reproduced, stored in an electronic system, or transmitted in any form or by any means, electronic, mechanical, photocopy, recording, or otherwise, without the prior permission of the copyright owner.

Printed in the United States of America

88 89 90 91 92 / LP / 8 7 6 5 4

*Jesus' people are called
to love and to adore God.
This booklet is for those
who love the Lord.
It will help you express your love
in worship and praise.
It draws together Scripture to
guide you:
to guide you to prepare your heart
for praise,
to guide you with biblical patterns
of praise,
and to guide you with God's own
priorities in praise.*

Contents

Introduction 9

Part One: Preparation for Praise
Eighty-seven passages for meditation to prepare your heart to praise the Lord. 13

Part Two: Patterns for Praise
For Answered Prayer 29
At the Red Sea 30
For Deliverance 32
For God's Creation 34
For God's Sovereign Rule 35
For God's Power 36
For the Privilege of Worship 38
To God as Judge 39
For Forgiveness 40
For Healing 41
For Nature 42
For God's Enduring Love 44
For Personal Relationship 46
For God's Character 48
At History's End 50

Part Three: Priorities in Praise
God, the Faithful 53
God, the Loving 54
God, the Creator 55
God, the Almighty 56
God, Our Refuge 57

God, the Sovereign Lord   58
God, the Judge   59
God, the Forgiving   60
God, the Merciful   61
God, the Sustainer   62
God, the Miracle Worker   63
God, the Gracious   64
God, the Spirit   65
God, the Healer   66
Jesus, the Servant   67
God, the Just   68
God, the Righteous   69
God, My Guide   71
God, the Savior   72
God, the Good   73
Jesus, the Son   74
Christ, the Lord   75
Personal Praise Passages   77

Introduction

Jesus spoke gently to the woman at the well. John tells us that Christ led this Samaritan woman to personal faith and taught her about worship. "A time is coming," Jesus said, "when the true worshipers will worship the Father in spirit and in truth, for they are the kind of worshipers the Father seeks. God is spirit, and his worshipers must worship in spirit and in truth" (John 4:23–24).

The age of the Spirit is with us, and with the Holy Spirit to aid us, you and I are invited to worship. We lift up our hearts and our spirits to the Lord, with worship shaped by his truth, to praise the Lord.

This booklet has three sections. Each will enrich your times of worship and praise. In each section, the Bible alone speaks to you, guiding your thoughts and your heart.

The first section has passages that will help you prepare for worship. These words are for meditation, to focus your thoughts on the Lord and on your own relationship with him.

The second section contains examples of extended passages of praise. The patterns found here in the praise given God by Bible men and women will tune your own heart to the nature and the wonder of praise.

The third section focuses on the Lord. It selects Old and New Testament verses which remind us of who our God is. Reading it, our hearts are filled with the realization of how great are God's love, mercy, wisdom, and other wonderful attributes. With our hearts and minds filled with the Lord, we are ready to praise God for who he by nature is. This is the intimate heart of praise: to bless God for who he is, and to express our love-filled awe at the beauty of our God.

PART ONE

Preparation for Praise

How do we ready ourselves to worship? One way is by meditation. We focus on words of Scripture which tune our hearts to the Lord. This first section of the Believer's Praise Book contains eighty-seven passages for meditation. Read them prayerfully. Let the Lord speak to you through those that help you sense his presence. You'll find that several of these passages will be particularly precious to you. Circle them. Then, as you take time to worship, return to them. Read, meditate, and let the Holy Spirit lift your heart up to the Lord.

PREPARATION FOR PRAISE

Acknowledge and take to heart this day that the Lord is God in heaven above and on the earth below. There is no other.
Deuteronomy 4:39

The Lord did not set his affection on you and choose you because you were more numerous than other peoples, for you were the fewest of all peoples. But it was because the Lord loved you and kept the oath he swore to your forefathers . . . Know therefore that the Lord your God is God; he is the faithful God, keeping his covenant of love to a thousand generations of those who love him and keep his commands. *Deuteronomy 7:7–9*

To the Lord your God belong the heavens, even the highest heavens, the earth and everything in it. Yet the Lord set his affection on your forefathers and loved them, and he chose you.
Deuteronomy 10:14–15

O Lord, God of Israel, there is no God like you in heaven above or on earth below—you who keep your covenant of love with your servants who continue wholeheartedly in your way. *1 Kings 8:23*

O Lord, God of Israel, enthroned between the cherubim, you alone are God over all the kingdoms of the earth. You have made heaven and earth. Give ear, O Lord, and hear; open your eyes, O Lord, and see. *2 Kings 19:15–16*

PREPARATION FOR PRAISE

Give thanks to the LORD, call on his name; make known among the nations what he has done. Sing to him, sing praise to him; tell of all his wonderful acts.
1 Chronicles 16:8–9

Glory in his holy name; let the hearts of those who seek the LORD rejoice. Look to the LORD and his strength; seek his face always. *1 Chronicles 16:10–11*

Praise be to you, O LORD, God of our father Israel, from everlasting to everlasting.

Yours, O LORD, is the greatness and the power and the glory and the majesty and the splendor, for everything in heaven and earth is yours.

Yours, O LORD, is the kingdom; you are exalted as head over all.

Wealth and honor come from you; you are the ruler of all things.

In your hands are strength and power to exalt and give strength to all.

Now, our God, we give you thanks, and praise your glorious name.
1 Chronicles 29:10–13

Blessed be your glorious name, and may it be exalted above all blessing and praise. You alone are the LORD. You made the heavens, even the highest heavens, and all their starry host, the earth and all that is on it, the seas and all that is in them. You give life to everything, and the multitudes of heaven worship you. *Nehemiah 9:5–6*

PREPARATION FOR PRAISE

But I, by your great mercy, will come into your house; in reverence will I bow down toward your holy temple. *Psalm 5:7*

But let all who take refuge in you be glad; let them ever sing for joy. Spread your protection over them, that those who love your name may rejoice in you.
Psalm 5:11

I will praise you, O Lord, with all my heart; I will tell of all your wonders. I will be glad and rejoice in you; I will sing praise to your name, O Most High.
Psalm 9:1–2

You have made known to me the path of life; you will fill me with joy in your presence, with eternal pleasures at your right hand. *Psalm 16:11*

I love you, O Lord my strength. The Lord is my rock, my fortress and my deliverer; my God is my rock, in whom I take refuge. He is my shield and the horn of my salvation, my stronghold. I call to the Lord who is worthy of praise, and I am saved from my enemies. *Psalm 18:1–3*

May the words of my mouth and the meditation of my heart be pleasing in your sight, O Lord, my Rock and my Redeemer.
Psalm 19:14

To you, O Lord, I lift up my soul; in you I trust, O my God. *Psalm 25:1*

One thing I ask of the Lord, this is what I seek: that I may dwell in the house of the

PREPARATION FOR PRAISE

L‍ORD all the days of my life, to gaze upon the beauty of the L‍ORD. *Psalm 27:4*

My heart says of you, "Seek his face!" Your face, L‍ORD, I will seek. *Psalm 27:8*

Ascribe to the L‍ORD, O mighty ones, ascribe to the L‍ORD glory and strength. Ascribe to the L‍ORD the glory due his name; worship the L‍ORD in the splendor of his holiness. *Psalm 29:1–2*

Praise be to the L‍ORD, for he showed his wonderful love to me. *Psalm 31:21*

Sing joyfully to the L‍ORD, you righteous; it is fitting for the upright to praise him. Praise the L‍ORD with the harp; make music to him on the ten-stringed lyre. Sing to him a new song; play skillfully, and shout for joy. *Psalm 33:1–3*

I will extol the L‍ORD at all times; his praise will always be on my lips. My soul will boast in the L‍ORD; let the afflicted hear and rejoice. Glorify the L‍ORD with me; let us exalt his name together. *Psalm 34:1–3*

My whole being will exclaim, "Who is like you, O L‍ORD?" *Psalm 35:10*

As the deer pants for streams of water, so my soul pants for you, O God. My soul thirsts for God, for the living God. When can I go and meet with God? *Psalm 42:1–2*

By day the L‍ORD directs his love, at night his song is with me—a prayer to the God of my life. *Psalm 42:8*

PREPARATION FOR PRAISE

Be still and know that I am God; I will be exalted among the nations, I will be exalted in the earth. *Psalm 46:10*

Clap your hands, all you nations; shout to God with cries of joy. How awesome is the LORD Most High, the great King over all the earth! *Psalm 47:1–2*

God has ascended amid shouts of joy, the LORD amid the sounding of trumpets. Sing praises to God, sing praises; sing praises to our King, sing praises. For God is the King of all the earth; sing to him a psalm of praise. *Psalm 47:5–7*

Within your temple, O God, we meditate on your unfailing love. Like your name, O God, your praise reaches to the ends of the earth; your right hand is filled with righteousness. *Psalm 48:9–10*

I will praise you forever for what you have done; in your name I will hope, for your name is good. I will praise you in the presence of your saints. *Psalm 52:9*

I will sacrifice a freewill offering to you; I will praise your name, O LORD, for it is good. *Psalm 54:6*

I will praise you, O Lord, among the nations; I will sing of you among the peoples. For great is your love, reaching to the heavens; your faithfulness reaches to the skies. Be exalted, O God, above the heavens; let your glory be over all the earth. *Psalm 57:9–11*

PREPARATION FOR PRAISE

I will sing of your strength, in the morning I will sing of your love; for you are my fortress, my refuge in times of trouble. O my Strength, I sing praise to you; you, O God, are my fortress, my loving God. *Psalm 59:16–17*

O God, you are my God, earnestly I seek you; my soul thirsts for you, my body longs for you, in a dry and weary land where there is no water. *Psalm 63:1*

I will praise you as long as I live, and in your name I will lift up my hands.
Psalm 63:4

Praise awaits you, O God, in Zion; to you our vows will be fulfilled. O you who hear prayer, to you all men will come.
Psalm 65:1–2

Shout with joy to God, all the earth! Sing to the glory of his name; offer him glory and praise! Say to God, "How awesome are your deeds!" *Psalm 66:1–3*

Sing to God, sing praise to his name, extol him who rides on the clouds—his name is the LORD—and rejoice before him.
Psalm 68:4

Sing to God, O kingdoms of the earth, sing praises to the Lord, to him who rides the ancient skies above, who thunders with mighty voice. Proclaim the power of God, whose majesty is over Israel, whose power is in the skies. You are awesome, O God, in your sanctuary; the God of Israel

PREPARATION FOR PRAISE

gives power and strength to his people. Praise be to God! *Psalm 68:32–35*

I will praise God's name in song and glorify him with thanksgiving. This will please the Lord more than an ox, more than a bull with its horns and hoofs. The poor will see and be glad—you who seek God, may your hearts live!
Psalm 69:30–32

Be my rock of refuge, to which I can always go. *Psalm 71:3*

But as for me, I will always have hope; I will praise you more and more. My mouth will tell of your righteousness, of your salvation all day long, though I know not its measure. *Psalm 71:14–15*

I will praise you with the harp for your faithfulness, O my God; I will sing praise to you with the lyre, O Holy One of Israel. My lips will shout for joy when I sing praise to you—I, whom you have redeemed. *Psalm 71:22–23*

Praise be to the Lord God, the God of Israel, who alone does marvelous deeds. Praise be to his glorious name forever; may the whole earth be filled with his glory. Amen and Amen. *Psalm 72:18–19*

How lovely is your dwelling place, O Lord Almighty! My soul yearns, even faints for the courts of the Lord; my heart and my flesh cry out for the living God.
Psalm 84:1–2

PREPARATION FOR PRAISE

Blessed are those who dwell in your house; they are ever praising you.
Psalm 84:4

Blessed are those whose strength is in you, who have their hearts set on pilgrimage . . . They go from strength to strength till each appears before God in Zion.
Psalm 84:5, 7

Bring joy to your servant, for to you, O Lord, I lift up my soul. *Psalm 86:4*

Teach me your way, O LORD, and I will walk in your truth; give me an undivided heart, that I may fear your name. I will praise you, O Lord my God, with all my heart; I will glorify your name forever. For great is your love toward me; you have delivered my soul from the depths of the grave. *Psalm 86:11–13*

I will sing of the LORD'S great love forever; . . . I will declare that your love stands firm forever. *Psalm 89:1–2*

The heavens praise your wonders, O LORD, your faithfulness too, in the assembly of the holy ones. For who in the skies above can compare with the LORD? Who is like the LORD among the heavenly beings? In the council of the holy ones God is greatly feared; he is more awesome than all who surround him. O LORD God Almighty, who is like you? You are mighty, O LORD, and your faithfulness surrounds you.
Psalm 89:5–8

PREPARATION FOR PRAISE

Blessed are those who have learned to acclaim you, who walk in the light of your presence, O Lord. *Psalm 89:15*

It is good to praise the Lord and make music to your name, O Most High, to proclaim your love in the morning and your faithfulness at night, to the music of the ten-stringed lyre and the melody of the harp. For you make me glad by your deeds, O Lord; I sing for joy at the works of your hands. How great are your works, O Lord, how profound your thoughts!
Psalm 92:1−5

Come, let us sing for joy to the Lord; let us shout aloud to the Rock of our salvation. Let us come before him with thanksgiving and extol him with music and song. For the Lord is the great God, the great King above all gods. *Psalm 95:1−3*

Come, let us bow down in worship, let us kneel before the Lord our Maker; for he is our God and we are the people of his pasture, the flock under his care.
Psalm 95:6−7

Sing to the Lord a new song; sing to the Lord, all the earth. Sing to the Lord, praise his name; proclaim his salvation day after day. Declare his glory among the nations, his marvelous deeds among all peoples.
Psalm 96:1−3

Great is the Lord and most worthy of praise. *Psalm 96:4*

PREPARATION FOR PRAISE

Worship the Lord in the splendor of his holiness; tremble before him, all the earth.
Psalm 96:9

Shout for joy to the Lord, all the earth, burst into jubilant song with music; make music to the Lord with the harp, with the harp and the sound of singing, with trumpets and the blast of the ram's horn—shout for joy before the Lord, the King.
Psalm 98:4–6

Know that the Lord is God. It is he who has made us, and we are his; we are his people, the sheep of his pasture.
Psalm 100:3

Enter his gates with thanksgiving and his courts with praise; give thanks to him and praise his name. For the Lord is good and his love endures forever.
Psalm 100:4–5

Praise the Lord, O my soul; all my inmost being, praise his holy name. Praise the Lord, O my soul, and forget not all his benefits. *Psalm 103:1–2*

I will sing to the Lord all my life; I will sing praise to my God as long as I live. May my meditation be pleasing to him, as I rejoice in the Lord. . . . Praise the Lord, O my soul. Praise the Lord.
Psalm 104:33–35

Sing to him, sing praise to him; tell of all his wonderful acts. Glory in his holy name; let the hearts of those who seek the Lord rejoice. *Psalm 105:2–3*

PREPARATION FOR PRAISE

I will praise you, O LORD, among the nations; I will sing of you among the peoples. For great is your love, higher than the heavens; your faithfulness reaches to the skies. Be exalted, O God, above the heavens, and let your glory be over all the earth. *Psalm 108:3–5*

Praise the LORD. Praise, O servants of the LORD, praise the name of the LORD. Let the name of the LORD be praised, both now and forevermore. From the rising of the sun to the place where it sets the name of the LORD is to be praised. *Psalm 113:1–3*

Not to us, O LORD, not to us but to your name be the glory, because of your love and faithfulness. *Psalm 115:1*

I have sought your face with all my heart; be gracious to me according to your promise. *Psalm 119:58*

Praise the LORD, for the LORD is good; sing praise to his name, for that is pleasant. For the LORD has chosen Jacob to be his own, Israel to be his treasured possession. I know that the LORD is great, that our Lord is greater than all gods. *Psalm 135:3–5*

I will praise you, O LORD, with all my heart; before the "gods" I will sing your praise. I will bow down toward your holy temple and will praise your name for your love and your faithfulness, for you have exalted above all things your name and your word. *Psalm 138:1–2*

PREPARATION FOR PRAISE

I will exalt you, my God the King; I will praise your name for ever and ever. Every day I will praise you and extol your name for ever and ever. Great is the LORD and most worthy of praise; his greatness no one can fathom. *Psalm 145:1–3*

Praise the LORD. How good it is to sing praises to our God, how pleasant and fitting to praise him! *Psalm 147:1*

Let them praise the name of the LORD, for his name alone is exalted; his splendor is above the earth and the heavens.
Psalm 148:13

Praise the LORD. Praise God in his sanctuary; praise him in his mighty heavens. Praise him for his acts of power; praise him for his surpassing greatness. Praise him with the sounding of the trumpet, praise him with the harp and lyre, praise him with tambourine and dancing, praise him with the strings and flute, praise him with the clash of cymbals, praise him with resounding cymbals. Let everything that has breath praise the LORD. Praise the LORD. *Psalm 150:1–6*

Give thanks to the LORD, call on his name; make known among the nations what he has done, and proclaim that his name is exalted. Sing to the LORD, for he has done glorious things; let this be known to all the world. Shout aloud and sing for joy, people of Zion, for great is the Holy One of Israel among you. *Isaiah 12:4–6*

PREPARATION FOR PRAISE

My soul praises the Lord and my spirit rejoices in God my Savior, for he has been mindful of the humble state of his servant.
Luke 1:46–48

Oh, the depth of the riches of the wisdom and knowledge of God! How unsearchable his judgments, and his paths beyond tracing out! Who has known the mind of the Lord? Or who has been his counselor? Who has ever given to God, that God should repay him? For from him and through him and to him are all things. To him be the glory forever! Amen.
Romans 11:33–36

Now to him who is able to do immeasurably more than all we ask or imagine, according to his power that is at work within us, to him be glory in the church and in Christ Jesus throughout all generations, for ever and ever! Amen.
Ephesians 3:20–21

Now to the King eternal, immortal, invisible, the only God, be honor and glory for ever and ever. Amen. *1 Timothy 1:17*

Through Jesus, therefore, let us continually offer to God a sacrifice of praise—the fruit of lips that confess his name.
Hebrews 13:15

To him who is able to keep you from falling and to present you before his glorious presence without fault and with great joy—to the only God our Savior be glory, majesty, power and authority, through

PREPARATION FOR PRAISE

Jesus Christ our Lord, before all ages, now and forevermore! Amen. *Jude 24–25*

To him who loves us and has freed us from our sins by his blood, and has made us to be a kingdom and priests to serve his God and Father—to him be glory and power for ever and ever! Amen.
Revelation 1:5–6

You are worthy, our Lord and God, to receive glory and honor and power, for you created all things, and by your will they were created and have their being.
Revelation 4:11

Worthy is the Lamb, who was slain, to receive power and wealth and wisdom and strength and honor and glory and praise!
Revelation 5:12

To him who sits on the throne and to the Lamb be praise and honor and glory and power, for ever and ever! *Revelation 5:13*

Amen! Praise and glory and wisdom and thanks and honor and power and strength be to our God for ever and ever. Amen!
Revelation 7:12

Hallelujah! For our Lord God Almighty reigns. Let us rejoice and be glad and give him glory! *Revelation 19:6–7*

PART TWO

Patterns for Praise

How do you and I praise the Lord? The Bible is rich in expressions of praise by God's people. We can learn to praise by tuning our hearts to the adoration they express. We can discover the joy of remembering God's works and visualizing his greatness as we speak to him with words of heartfelt acclamation.

FOR ANSWERED PRAYER

My heart rejoices in the Lord; in the Lord my horn is lifted high. My mouth boasts over my enemies for I delight in your deliverance. There is no one holy like the Lord; there is no one besides you; there is no Rock like our God. Do not keep talking so proudly or let your mouth speak such arrogance, for the Lord is a God who knows, and by him deeds are weighed. The bows of the warriors are broken, but those who stumbled are armed with strength. Those who were full hire themselves out for food, but those who were hungry hunger no more. She who was barren has borne seven children, but she who has had many sons pines away. The Lord brings death and makes alive; he brings down to the grave and raises up. The Lord sends poverty and wealth; he humbles and he exalts. He raises the poor from the dust and lifts the needy from the ash heap; he seats them with princes and has them inherit a throne of honor. For the foundations of the earth are the Lord's; upon them he has set the world. He will guard the feet of his saints, but the wicked will be silenced in darkness. It is not by strength that one prevails; those who oppose the Lord will be shattered. He will thunder against them from heaven; the Lord will judge the ends of the earth. He will give strength to his king and exalt the horn of his anointed. *1 Samuel 2*

AT THE RED SEA

I will sing to the Lord, for he is highly exalted. The horse and its rider he has hurled into the sea. The Lord is my strength and my song; he has become my salvation. He is my God, and I will praise him, my father's God, and I will exalt him. The Lord is a warrior; the Lord is his name. Pharaoh's chariots and his army he has hurled into the sea. The best of Pharaoh's officers are drowned in the Red Sea. The deep waters have covered them; they sank to the depths like a stone. Your right hand, O Lord, was majestic in power. Your right hand, O Lord, shattered the enemy. In the greatness of your majesty you threw down those who opposed you. You unleashed your burning anger; it consumed them like stubble. By the blast of your nostrils the waters piled up. The surging waters stood firm like a wall; the deep waters congealed in the heart of the sea. The enemy boasted, "I will pursue, I will overtake them. I will divide the spoils; I will gorge myself on them. I will draw my sword and my hand will destroy them." But you blew with your breath, and the sea covered them. They sank like lead in the mighty waters. Who among the gods is like you, O Lord? Who is like you— majestic in holiness, awesome in glory, working wonders? You stretched out your right hand and the earth swallowed them. In your unfailing love you will lead the people you have redeemed. In your strength you will guide them to your holy dwelling. The nations will hear and tremble; anguish will

AT THE RED SEA

grip the people of Philistia. The chiefs of Edom will be terrified, the leaders of Moab will be seized with trembling. the people of Canaan will melt away; terror and dread will fall upon them. By the power of your arm they will be as still as a stone—until your people pass by, O LORD, until the people you bought pass by. You will bring them in and plant them on the mountain of your inheritance—the place, O LORD, you made for your dwelling, the sanctuary, O LORD, your hands established. The LORD will reign for ever and ever. *Exodus 15*

FOR DELIVERANCE

The LORD is my rock, my fortress and my deliverer; my God is my rock, in whom I take refuge, my shield and the horn of my salvation. He is my stronghold, my refuge and my savior—from violent men you save me. I call to the LORD, who is worthy of praise, and I am saved from my enemies. The waves of death swirled about me; the torrents of destruction overwhelmed me. The cords of the grave coiled about me; the snares of death confronted me. In my distress I called to the LORD; I called out to my God. From his temple he heard my voice; my cry came to his ears. The earth trembled and quaked, the foundations of the heavens shook; they trembled because he was angry. Smoke rose from his nostrils; consuming fire came from his mouth, burning coals blazed out of it. He parted the heavens and came down; dark clouds were under his feet. He mounted on cherubim and flew; he soared on the wings of the wind. He made darkness his canopy around him—the dark rain clouds of the sky. Out of the brightness of his presence bolts of lightning blazed forth. The LORD thundered from heaven; the voice of the Most High resounded. He shot arrows and scattered the enemies, bolts of lightning and routed them. The valleys of the sea were exposed and the foundations of the earth laid bare at the rebuke of the LORD, at the blast of breath from his nostrils. He reached down from on high and took hold of me; he drew me out of deep waters. He rescued me from my powerful enemy,

FOR DELIVERANCE

from my foes, who were too strong for me. They confronted me in the day of my disaster, but the LORD was my support. He brought me out into a spacious place; he rescued me because he delighted in me. The LORD has dealt with me according to my righteousness; according to the cleanness of my hands he has rewarded me. For I have kept the ways of the LORD; I have not done evil by turning from my God. All his laws are before me; I have not turned away from his decrees. I have been blameless before him and have kept myself from sin. The LORD has rewarded me according to my righteousness, according to my cleanness in his sight.... As for God, his way is perfect; the word of the LORD is flawless. He is a shield for all who take refuge in him.... The LORD lives! Praise be to my Rock! Exalted be God, the Rock, my Savior! He is the God who avenges me, who puts nations under me, who sets me free from my enemies. You exalted me above my foes; from violent men you rescued me. Therefore I will praise you, O LORD, among the nations; I will sing praises to your name.

2 Samuel 22:2–25, 31, 47–50

FOR GOD'S CREATION

O Lord, our Lord, how majestic is your name in all the earth! You have set your glory above the heavens. From the lips of children and infants you have ordained praise because of your enemies, to silence the foe and the avenger. When I consider your heavens, the work of your fingers, the moon and the stars, which you have set in place, what is man that you are mindful of him, the son of man that you care for him? You made him a little lower than the heavenly beings and crowned him with glory and honor. You made him ruler over the works of your hands; you put all things under his feet: all flocks and herds, and the beasts of the field, the birds of the air, and the fish of the sea, all that swim in the paths of the seas. O Lord, our Lord, how majestic is your name in all the earth!

Psalm 8

FOR GOD'S SOVEREIGN RULE

Clap your hands, all you nations; shout to God with cries of joy. How awesome is the LORD Most High, the great King over all the earth! He subdued nations under us, peoples under our feet. He chose our inheritance for us, the pride of Jacob, whom he loved. God has ascended amid shouts of joy, the LORD amid the sounding of trumpets. Sing praises to God, sing praises; sing praises to our King, sing praises. For God is the King of all the earth; sing to him a psalm of praise. God reigns over the nations; God is seated on his holy throne. The nobles of the nations assemble as the people of the God of Abraham, for the kings of the earth belong to God; he is greatly exalted.   *Psalm 47*

FOR GOD'S POWER

May God arise, may his enemies be scattered; may his foes flee before him. As smoke is blown away by the wind, may you blow them away; as wax melts before the fire, may the wicked perish before God. But may the righteous be glad and rejoice before God; may they be happy and joyful. Sing to God, sing praise to his name, extol him who rides on the clouds—his name is the LORD—and rejoice before him. A father to the fatherless, a defender of widows, is God in his holy dwelling. God sets the lonely in families, he leads forth the prisoners with singing; but the rebellious live in a sun-scorched land. When you went out before your people, O God, when you marched through the wasteland, the earth shook, the heavens poured down rain, before God, the One of Sinai, before God, the God of Israel. You gave abundant showers, O God; you refreshed your weary inheritance. Your people settled in it, and from your bounty, O God, you provided for the poor. The Lord announced the word, and great was the company of those who proclaimed it: .... The chariots of God are tens of thousands and thousands of thousands; the Lord has come from Sinai into his sanctuary. Praise be to the Lord, to God our Savior, who daily bears our burdens. Our God is a God who saves; from the Sovereign LORD comes escape from death. Surely God will crush the heads of his enemies, the hairy crowns of those who go on in their sins. Summon your power, O God; show us your strength,

FOR GOD'S POWER

O God, as you have done before. Because of your temple at Jerusalem kings will bring you gifts. Rebuke the beast among the reeds, the herd of bulls among the calves of the nations. Humbled, may it bring bars of silver. Scatter the nations who delight in war. Envoys will come from Egypt; Cush will submit herself to God. Sing to God, O kingdoms of the earth, sing praises to the Lord, to him who rides the ancient skies above, who thunders with mighty voice. Proclaim the power of God, whose majesty is over Israel, whose power is in the skies. You are awesome, O God, in your sanctuary; the God of Israel gives power and strength to his people. Praise be to God!

Psalm 68:1–11, 17, 19–21, 28–35

FOR THE PRIVILEGE OF WORSHIP

How lovely is your dwelling place, O Lord Almighty! My soul yearns, even faints for the courts of the Lord; my heart and my flesh cry out for the living God. Even the sparrow has found a home, and the swallow a nest for herself, where she may have her young—a place near your altar, O Lord Almighty, my King and my God. Blessed are those who dwell in your house; they are ever praising you. Blessed are those whose strength is in you, who have set their hearts on pilgrimage. As they pass through the Valley of Baca, they make it a place of springs; the autumn rains also cover it with pools. They go from strength to strength till each appears before God in Zion. Hear my prayer, O Lord God Almighty; listen to me, O God of Jacob. Look upon our shield, O God; look with favor on your anointed one. Better is one day in your courts than a thousand elsewhere; I would rather be a doorkeeper in the house of my God than dwell in the tents of the wicked. For the Lord God is a sun and shield; the Lord bestows favor and honor; no good thing does he withhold from those whose walk is blameless—O Lord Almighty, blessed is the man who trusts in you. *Psalm 84*

TO GOD AS JUDGE

Sing to the Lord a new song; sing to the Lord, all the earth. Sing to the Lord, praise his name; proclaim his salvation day after day. Declare his glory among the nations, his marvelous deeds among all peoples. For great is the Lord and most worthy of praise; he is to be feared above all gods. For all the gods of the nations are idols, but the Lord made the heavens. Splendor and majesty are before him; strength and glory are in his sanctuary. Ascribe to the Lord, O families of nations, ascribe to the Lord glory and strength. Ascribe to the Lord the glory due his name; bring an offering and come into his courts. Worship the Lord in the splendor of his holiness; tremble before him, all the earth. Say among the nations, "The Lord reigns." The world is firmly established, it cannot be moved; he will judge his peoples with equity. Let the heavens rejoice, let the earth be glad; let the sea resound, and all that is in it; let the fields be jubilant, and everything in them. Then all the trees of the forest will sing for joy; they will sing before the Lord, for he comes, he comes to judge the earth. He will judge the world in righteousness and the peoples in truth.

Psalm 96

FOR FORGIVENESS

Praise the Lord, O my soul; all my inmost being, praise his holy name. Praise the Lord, O my soul, and forget not all his benefits. He forgives all my sins and heals all my diseases; he redeems my life from the pit and crowns me with love and compassion. He satisfies my desires with good things, so that my youth is renewed like the eagle's. The Lord works righteousness and justice for all the oppressed. He made known his ways to Moses, his deeds to the people of Israel: The Lord is compassionate and gracious, slow to anger, abounding in love. He will not always accuse, nor will he harbor his anger forever; he does not treat us as our sins deserve or repay us according to our iniquities. For as high as the heavens are above the earth, so great is his love for those who fear him; as far as the east is from the west, so far has he removed our transgressions from us. As a father has compassion on his children, so the Lord has compassion on those who fear him; for he knows how we are formed, he remembers that we are dust. . . . Praise the Lord, all his heavenly hosts, you his servants who do his will. Praise the Lord, all his works, everywhere in his dominion. Praise the Lord, O my soul.

Psalm 103: 1–14, 21–22

FOR HEALING

I said, "In the prime of my life must I go through the gates of death and be robbed of the rest of my years?" I said, "I will not again see the LORD, the LORD, in the land of the living; no longer will I look on mankind, or be with those who now dwell in this world. Like a shepherd's tent my house has been pulled down and taken from me.... My eyes grew weak as I looked to the heavens. I am troubled; O Lord, come to my aid!" But what can I say? He has spoken to me, and he himself has done this. I will walk humbly all my years because of the anguish of my soul. Lord, by such things men live; and my spirit finds life in them too. You restored me to health and let me live. Surely it was for my benefit that I suffered such anguish. In your love you kept me from the pit of destruction; you have put all my sins behind your back. For the grave cannot praise you, death cannot sing your praise; those who go down to the pit cannot hope for your faithfulness. The living, the living—they praise you, as I am doing today.... The LORD will save me, and we will sing with stringed instruments all the days of our lives in the temple of the LORD. *Isaiah 38:10–12, 14–20*

FOR NATURE

Praise the LORD, O my soul. O LORD my God, you are very great; you are clothed with splendor and majesty. He wraps himself in light as with a garment; he stretches out the heavens like a tent and lays the beams of his upper chambers on their waters. He makes the clouds his chariot and rides on the wings of the wind. He makes winds his messengers, flames of fire his servants. He set the earth on its foundations; it can never be moved. You covered it with the deep as with a garment; the waters stood above the mountains. But at your rebuke the waters fled, at the sound of your thunder they took to flight; they flowed over the mountains, they went down into the valleys, to the place you assigned for them. You set a boundary they cannot cross; never again will they cover the earth. He makes springs pour water into the ravines; it flows between the mountains. They give water to all the beasts of the field; the wild donkeys quench their thirst. The birds of the air nest by the waters; they sing among the branches. He waters the mountains from his upper chambers; the earth is satisfied by the fruit of his work. He makes grass grow for the cattle, and plants for man to cultivate—bringing forth food from the earth: wine that gladdens the heart of man, oil to make his face shine, and bread that sustains his heart. The trees of the LORD are well watered, the cedars of Lebanon that he planted. There the birds make their nests; the stork has its home in the pine

FOR NATURE

trees. The high mountains belong to the wild goats; the crags are a refuge for the coneys. The moon marks off the seasons, and the sun knows when to go down. You bring darkness, it becomes night, and all the beasts of the forest prowl. The lions roar for their prey and seek their food from God. The sun rises, and they steal away; they return and lie down in their dens. Then man goes out to his work, to his labor until evening. How many are your works, O LORD! In wisdom you made them all; the earth is full of your creatures. . . . When you send your Spirit, they are created, and you renew the face of the earth. May the glory of the LORD endure forever; may the LORD rejoice in his works. I will sing to the LORD all my life; I will sing praise to my God as long as I live. May my meditation be pleasing to him, as I rejoice in the LORD. Praise the LORD, O my soul. Praise the LORD.   *Psalm 104:1–24, 30–31, 33–35*

FOR GOD'S ENDURING LOVE

Give thanks to the LORD, for he is good. *His love endures forever.* Give thanks to the God of gods. *His love endures forever.* Give thanks to the Lord of lords: *His love endures forever.* to him who alone does great wonders, *His love endures forever.* who by his understanding made the heavens, *His love endures forever.* who spread out the earth upon the waters, *His love endures forever.* who made the great lights—*His love endures forever.* the sun to govern the day, *His love endures forever.* the moon and stars to govern the night; *His love endures forever.* to him who struck down the firstborn of Egypt *His love endures forever.* and brought Israel out from among them *His love endures forever.* with a mighty hand and outstretched arm; *His love endures forever.* to him who divided the Red Sea asunder *His love endures forever.* and brought Israel through the midst of it, *His love endures forever.* but swept Pharaoh and his army into the Red Sea; *His love endures forever.* to him who led his people through the desert, *His love endures forever.* who struck down great kings, *His love endures forever.* and killed mighty kings—*His love endures forever.* Sihon king of the Amorites *His love endures forever.* and Og king of Bashan—*His love endures forever.* and gave their land as an inheritance, *His love endures forever.* an inheritance to his servant Israel; *His love endures forever.* to the One who remembered us in our low estate *His love endures forever.* and freed

FOR GOD'S ENDURING LOVE

us from our enemies, *His love endures forever.* and who gives food to every creature. *His love endures forever.* Give thanks to the God of heaven. *His love endures forever.*   *Psalm 136*

FOR PERSONAL RELATIONSHIP

O Lord, you have searched me and you know me. You know when I sit and when I rise; you perceive my thoughts from afar. You discern my going out and my lying down; you are familiar with all my ways. Before a word is on my tongue you know it completely, O Lord. You hem me in—behind and before; you have laid your hand upon me. Such knowledge is too wonderful for me, too lofty for me to attain. Where can I go from your Spirit? When can I flee from your presence? If I go up to the heavens, you are there; if I make my bed in the depths, you are there. If I rise on the wings of the dawn, if I settle on the far side of the sea, even there your hand will guide me, your right hand will hold me fast. If I say, "Surely the darkness will hide me and the light become night around me," even the darkness will not be dark to you; the night will shine like the day, for darkness is as light to you. For you created my inmost being; you knit me together in my mother's womb. I praise you because I am fearfully and wonderfully made; your works are wonderful, I know that full well. My frame was not hidden from you when I was made in the secret place. When I was woven together in the depths of the earth, your eyes saw my unformed body. All the days ordained for me were written in your book before one of them came to be. How precious to me are your thoughts, O God! How vast is the sum of them! Were I to count them, they would outnumber the grains of sand.

FOR PERSONAL RELATIONSHIP

When I awake I am still with you. If only you would slay the wicked, O God! Away from me, you bloodthirsty men! They speak of you with evil intent; your adversaries misuse your name. Do I not hate those who hate you, O Lord, and abhor those who rise up against you? I have nothing but hatred for them; I count them my enemies. Search me, O God, and know my heart; test me and know my anxious thoughts. See if there is any offensive way in me, and lead me in the way everlasting.
Psalm 139

FOR GOD'S CHARACTER

I will exalt you, my God the King; I will praise your name for ever and ever. Every day I will praise you and extol your name for ever and ever. Great is the LORD and most worthy of praise; his greatness no one can fathom. One generation will commend your works to another; they will tell of your mighty acts. They will speak of the glorious splendor of your majesty, and I will meditate on your wonderful works. They will tell of the power of your awesome works, and I will proclaim your great deeds. They will celebrate your abundant goodness and joyfully sing of your righteousness. The LORD is gracious and compassionate, slow to anger and rich in love. The LORD is good to all; he has compassion on all he has made. All you have made will praise you, O LORD; your saints will extol you. They will tell of the glory of your kingdom and speak of your might, so that all men may know of your mighty acts and the glorious splendor of your kingdom. Your kingdom is an everlasting kingdom, and your dominion endures through all generations. The LORD is faithful to all his promises and loving toward all he has made. The LORD upholds all those who fall and lifts up all who are bowed down. The eyes of all look to you, and you give them their food at the proper time. You open your hand and satisfy the desires of every living thing. The LORD is righteous in all his ways and loving toward all he has made. The LORD is near to all who call on him, to all who call on him in truth. He

FOR GOD'S CHARACTER

fulfills the desires of those who fear him; he hears their cry and saves them. The Lord watches over all who love him, but all the wicked he will destroy. My mouth will speak in praise of the Lord. Let every creature praise his holy name for ever and ever. *Psalm 145*

PERSECUTION

Blessed are those who are persecuted because of righteousness, for theirs is the kingdom of heaven. *Matthew 5:10*

You intended to harm me, but God intended it for good to accomplish what is now being done, the saving of many lives. *Genesis 50:20*

I call to the Lord, who is worthy of praise, and I am saved from my enemies. *2 Samuel 22:4*

I have set the Lord always before me. Because he is at my right hand, I will not be shaken. *Psalm 16:8*

Many are the woes of the wicked, but the Lord's unfailing love surrounds the man who trusts in him. *Psalm 32:10*

Do not fret because of evil men or be envious of those who do wrong; for like the grass they will soon wither, like green plants they will soon die away. *Psalm 37:1–2*

The Lord works righteousness and justice for all the oppressed. *Psalm 103:6*

He rescues the life of the needy from the hands of the wicked. *Jeremiah 20:13*

He must turn from evil and do good; he must seek peace and pursue it. For the eyes of the Lord are on the righteous, and his ears are attentive to their prayer. *1 Peter 3:11–12*

I will contend with those who contend with you, and your children I will save.

Isaiah 49:25

The scepter of the wicked will not remain over the land allotted to the righteous.

Psalm 125:3

The oppressor will come to an end.

Isaiah 16:4

PART THREE

Priorities in Praise

The intimate heart of worship is discovered as we speak directly to God, praising him for who he is. Many passages of Scripture speak to us beautifully about God's nature. We meet him as the Faithful, the Loving, the Wonder-working God. Each fresh revelation of who God is stands as his special invitation to you and me to reflect on his nature and to express our adoration and our appreciation in praise.

GOD, THE FAITHFUL

God is not a man, that he should lie, nor a son of man, that he should change his mind. Does he speak and not act? Does he promise and not fulfill? *Numbers 23:19*

The heavens praise your wonders, O Lord, your faithfulness too, in the assembly of the holy ones. For who in the skies above can compare with the Lord? Who is like the Lord among the heavenly beings? In the council of the holy ones God is greatly feared; he is more awesome than all who surround him. O Lord God Almighty, who is like you? You are mighty, O Lord, and your faithfulness surrounds you.
Psalm 89:5–8

Know therefore that the Lord your God is God; he is the faithful God, keeping his covenant of love to a thousand generations of those who love him and keep his commandments. *Deuteronomy 7:9*

The Lord is faithful to all his promises and loving toward all he has made. The Lord upholds all those who fall and lifts up all who are bowed down. The eyes of all look to you, and you give them their food at the proper time. You open your hand and satisfy the desires of every living thing. *Psalm 145:13–16*

To the faithful you show yourself faithful, to the blameless you show yourself blameless. You, O Lord, keep my lamp burning; my God turns my darkness into light. *Psalm 18:25, 28*

GOD, THE LOVING

I have loved you with an everlasting love; I have drawn you with loving-kindness. I will build you up again and you will be rebuilt, O Virgin Israel. Again you will take up your tambourines and go out to dance with the joyful.
Jeremiah 31:3–4

Your love, O Lord, reaches to the heavens, your faithfulness to the skies.... O Lord, you preserve both man and beast. How priceless is your unfailing love!
Psalm 36:5–7

We are more than conquerors through him who loved us. For I am convinced that neither death nor life, neither angels nor demons, neither the present nor the future, nor any powers, neither height nor depth, nor anything else in all creation, will be able to separate us from the love of God that is in Christ Jesus our Lord.
Romans 8:37–39

I will praise you, O Lord, among the nations; I will sing of you among the peoples. For great is your love, higher than the heavens; your faithfulness reaches to the skies. Be exalted, O God, above the heavens, and let your glory be over all the earth. *Psalm 108:3–5*

Because your love is better than life, my lips will glorify you. I will praise you as long as I live, and in your name I will lift up my hands. *Psalm 63:4–5*

GOD, THE CREATOR

By the word of the LORD were the heavens made, their starry host by the breath of his mouth. He gathers the waters of the sea into jars; let all the earth fear the LORD; let all the people of the world revere him. For he spoke, and it came to be; he commanded, and it stood firm.

Psalm 33:6–9

Do you not know? Have you not heard? Has it not been told to you from the beginning? Have you not understood since the earth was founded? He sits enthroned above the circle of the earth, and its people are like grasshoppers.... "To whom will you compare me? Or who is my equal?" says the Holy One. Lift your eyes and look to the heavens: who created all these? He who brings out the starry host one by one, and calls them each by name. Because of his great power and mighty strength, not one of them is missing.

Isaiah 40:21–22, 25–26

This is what the LORD says—your Redeemer, who formed you in the womb: I am the LORD, who has made all things, who alone stretched out the heavens, who spread out the earth by myself.

Isaiah 44:24

You alone are the LORD. You made the heavens, even the highest heavens, and all their starry host, the earth and all that is on it, the seas and all that is in them. You give life to everything, and the multitudes of heaven worship you. *Nehemiah 9:6*

GOD, THE ALMIGHTY

For the LORD your God is God of gods and Lord of lords, the great God, mighty and awesome, who shows no partiality and accepts no bribes. *Deuteronomy 10:17*

The Lord Jesus Christ . . . by the power that enables him to bring everything under his control, will transform our lowly bodies so that they will be like his glorious body.
Philippians 3:20–21

For the LORD is the great God, the great King above all gods. In his hand are the depths of the earth, and the mountain peaks belong to him. The sea is his, for he made it, and his hands formed the dry land. Come, let us bow down in worship, let us kneel before the LORD our Maker; for he is our God and we are the people of his pasture, the flock under his care.
Psalm 95:3–7

No one is like you, O LORD; you are great, and your name is mighty in power. Who should not revere you, O King of the nations? This is your due.
Jeremiah 10:6–7

Now to him who is able to do immeasurably more than all we ask or imagine, according to his power that is at work within us, to him be glory in the church and in Christ Jesus throughout all generations, for ever and ever! Amen.
Ephesians 3:20–21

GOD, OUR REFUGE

You have been a refuge for the poor, a refuge for the needy in his distress, a shelter from the storm and a shade from the heat. For the breath of the ruthless is like a storm driving against a wall and like the heat of the desert. You silence the uproar of foreigners; as heat is reduced by the shadow of a cloud, so the song of the ruthless is stilled. *Isaiah 25:4–5*

God is our refuge and strength, an ever present help in trouble. Therefore we will not fear, though the earth give way and the mountains fall into the heart of the sea, though its waters roar and foam and the mountains quake with their surging.... The LORD Almighty is with us; the God of Jacob is our fortress. *Psalm 46:1–3, 7*

The eternal God is your refuge, and underneath are the everlasting arms. He will drive your enemy before you.... Blessed are you, O Israel! Who is like you, a people saved by the LORD? He is your shield and helper and your glorious sword. *Deuteronomy 33:27, 29*

As for God, his way is perfect; the word of the LORD is flawless. He is a shield for all who take refuge in him. *2 Samuel 22:31*

If you make the Most High your dwelling—even the LORD, who is my refuge—then no harm will befall you, no disaster will come near your tent. For he will command his angels concerning you to guard you in all your ways. *Psalm 91:9–11*

GOD, THE SOVEREIGN LORD

This is what the LORD says—Israel's King and Redeemer, the LORD Almighty: I am the first and I am the last; apart from me there is no God. Who then is like me? Let him proclaim it. Let him declare and lay out before me what has happened since I established my ancient people, and what is yet to come—yes, let him foretell what will come. Do not tremble, do not be afraid. Did I not proclaim this and foretell it long ago? You are my witnesses. Is there any God besides me? No, there is no other Rock; I know not one. *Isaiah 44:6–8*

Praise be to you, O LORD, God of our father Israel, from everlasting to everlasting. Yours, O LORD, is the greatness and the power and the glory and the majesty and the splendor, for everything in heaven and earth is yours. Yours, O LORD, is the kingdom; you are exalted as head over all.
1 Chronicles 29:10–11

For God is the King of all the earth; sing to him a psalm of praise. God reigns over the nations; God is seated on his holy throne . . . the kings of the earth belong to God; he is greatly exalted. *Psalm 47:7–9*

See, the Sovereign LORD comes with power, and his arm rules for him. See, his reward is with him, and his recompense accompanies him. He tends his flock like a shepherd: He gathers the lambs in his arms and carries them close to his heart.
Isaiah 40:10–11

GOD, THE JUDGE

See now that I myself am He! There is no god besides me. I put to death and I bring to life. I have wounded and I will heal, and no one can deliver from my hand. *Deuteronomy 32:39*

The LORD reigns forever; he has established his throne for judgment. He will judge the world in righteousness; he will govern the peoples with justice.
Psalm 9:7–8

The Son of Man is going to come in his Father's glory with his angels, and then he will reward each person according to what he has done. *Matthew 16:27*

I the LORD search the heart and examine the mind, to reward a man according to his conduct, according to what his deeds deserve. *Jeremiah 17:10*

Say among the nations, "The LORD reigns." The world is firmly established, it cannot be moved; he will judge the peoples with equity. Let the heavens rejoice, let the earth be glad; let the sea resound, and all that is in it; let the fields be jubilant, and everything in them. Then all the trees of the forest will sing for joy, they will sing before the LORD, for he comes, he comes to judge the earth. He will judge the world in righteousness and the peoples in his truth. *Psalm 96:10–13*

GOD, THE FORGIVING

Who is a God like you, who pardons sin and forgives the transgression of the remnant of his inheritance? You do not stay angry forever but delight to show mercy. You will again have compassion on us; you will tread our sins underfoot and hurl all our iniquities into the depths of the sea.
Micah 7:18–19

Praise the LORD, O my soul; all my inmost being, praise his holy name. Praise the LORD, O my soul, and forget not all his benefits. He forgives all my sins and heals all my diseases; he redeems my life from the pit and crowns me with love and compassion. *Psalm 103:1–4*

The Father. . .has qualified you to share in the inheritance of the saints in the kingdom of light. For he has rescued us from the dominion of darkness and brought us into the kingdom of the Son he loves, in whom we have redemption, the forgiveness of sins. *Colossians 1:12–14*

Then I acknowledged my sin to you and did not cover up my iniquity. I said, "I will confess my transgressions to the LORD"— and you forgave the guilt of my sin.
Psalm 32:5

If you, O LORD, kept a record of sins, O LORD, who could stand? But with you there is forgiveness; therefore you are feared.
Psalm 130:3–4

GOD, THE MERCIFUL

Praise be to the LORD, for he has heard my cry for mercy. The LORD is my strength and my shield; my heart trusts in him, and I am helped. My heart leaps for joy and I will give thanks to him in song.
Psalm 28:6–7

Praise be to the God and Father of our Lord Jesus Christ! In his great mercy he has given us a new birth into a living hope through the resurrection of Jesus Christ from the dead, and into an inheritance that can never perish, spoil or fade—kept in heaven for you. *1 Peter 1:3–4*

Shout for joy, O heavens; rejoice, O earth; burst into song, O mountains! For the LORD comforts his people and will have compassion on his afflicted ones . . . Can a mother forget the baby at her breast and have no compassion on the child she has borne? Though she may forget, I will not forget you! *Isaiah 49:13, 15*

You, O Lord, are a compassionate and gracious God, slow to anger, abounding in love and faithfulness. Turn to me and have mercy on me. . . . give me a sign of your goodness. *Psalm 86:15–17*

To you, O LORD, I called; to the Lord I cried for mercy: What gain is there in my destruction, in my going down into the pit? Will the dust praise you? . . . You turned my wailing into dancing . . . and clothed me with joy. *Psalm 30:8,11*

GOD, THE SUSTAINER

Do you not know? Have you not heard? The LORD is the everlasting God, the Creator of the ends of the earth. He will not grow tired or weary, and his understanding no one can fathom. He gives strength to the weary and increases the power of the weak. Even youths grow tired and weary, and young men stumble and fall; but those who hope in the LORD will renew their strength. They will soar on wings like eagles; they will run and not grow weary, they will walk and not be faint.
Isaiah 40:28–31

You care for the land and water it; you enrich it abundantly. The streams of God are filled with water to provide the people with grain, for so you have ordained it. You drench its furrows and level its ridges; you soften it with showers and bless its crops. You crown the year with your bounty, and your carts overflow with abundance.
Psalm 65:9–11

The LORD is exalted, for he dwells on high; he will fill Zion with justice and righteousness. He will be the sure foundation for your times, a rich store of salvation and wisdom and knowledge; the fear of the LORD is the key to this treasure.
Isaiah 33:5–6

The Son is the radiance of God's glory ... sustaining all things by his powerful word.
Hebrews 1:3

GOD, THE MIRACLE WORKER

Praise be to the LORD God, the God of Israel, who alone does marvelous deeds. Praise be to his glorious name forever; may the whole earth be filled with his glory. Amen and amen. *Psalm 72:18–19*

O LORD, you are my God; I will exalt you and praise your name, for in perfect faithfulness you have done marvelous things, things planned long ago. *Isaiah 25:1*

Great are the works of the LORD; they are pondered by all who delight in them. Glorious and majestic are his deeds, and his righteousness endures forever. He has caused his wonders to be remembered; the LORD is gracious and compassionate . . . He has shown his people the power of his works, giving them the lands of other nations. The works of his hands are faithful and just; all his precepts are trustworthy. They are steadfast for ever and ever, done in faithfulness and uprightness. He provided redemption for his people; he ordained his covenant forever—holy and awesome is his name. *Psalm 111:2–4, 6–9*

I will remember the deeds of the LORD; yes, I will remember your miracles of long ago. I will meditate on all your works and consider all your mighty deeds. Your ways, O God, are holy. What god is so great as our God? You are the God who performs miracles; you display your power among the peoples. With your mighty arm you redeemed your people. *Psalm 77:11–15*

GOD, THE GRACIOUS

The LORD is gracious and righteous; our God is full of compassion. The LORD protects the simplehearted; when I was in great need, he saved me. *Psalm 116:5–6*

Because of his great love for us, God, who is rich in mercy, made us alive with Christ even when we were dead in transgressions—it is by grace we have been saved. *Ephesians 2:4*

The God of all grace, who called you to his eternal glory in Christ, after you have suffered a little while, will himself restore you and make you strong, firm and steadfast. To him be the power for ever and ever. Amen. *1 Peter 5:10–11*

Grace and peace be yours in abundance through the knowledge of God and of Jesus our Lord. His divine power has given us everything we need for life and godliness through our knowledge of him.
2 Peter 1:2–3

It is by grace you have been saved, through faith—and this not from yourselves, it is the gift of God. *Ephesians 2:8*

But you, O Lord, are a compassionate and gracious God, slow to anger, abounding in love and faithfulness. *Psalm 86:15*

The LORD is gracious and compassionate, slow to anger and rich in love. The LORD is good to all. *Psalm 145:8*

GOD, THE SPIRIT

The Spirit is poured upon us from on high, and the desert becomes a fertile field, and the fertile field seems like a forest. Justice will dwell in the desert and righteousness live in the fertile field. The fruit of righteousness will be peace; the effect of righteousness will be quietness and confidence forever. *Isaiah 32:15–17*

Whoever believes in me, as the Scripture has said, streams of living water will flow from within him. By this he (Jesus) meant the Spirit, whom those who believed in him were later to receive.
John 7:38–39

In the last days, God says, I will pour out my Spirit on all people. Your sons and daughters will prophesy, your young men will see visions, your old men will dream dreams. Even on my servants, both men and women, I will pour out my Spirit in those days, and they will prophesy.
Acts 2:17–18

If the Spirit of him who raised Jesus from the dead is living in you, he who raised Christ from the dead will also give life to your mortal bodies through his Spirit, who lives in you. *Romans 8:11*

The Spirit himself testifies with our spirit that we are God's children.
Romans 8:16

When he, the Spirit of truth, comes, he will guide you into all truth. *John 16:13*

GOD, THE HEALER

Blessed is he who has regard for the weak; the LORD delivers him in times of trouble. The LORD will protect him and preserve his life; he will bless him in the land and not surrender him to the desire of his foes. The LORD will sustain him on his sickbed and restore him from his bed of illness. *Psalm 41:1–3*

Surely he took up our infirmities and carried our sorrows, yet we considered him stricken by God, smitten by him, and afflicted. But he was pierced for our transgressions, he was crushed for our iniquities; the punishment that brought us peace was upon him, and by his wounds we are healed. *Isaiah 53:4–5*

When the sun was setting, the people brought to Jesus all who had various kinds of sickness, and laying his hands on each one, he healed them. *Luke 4:40*

While Jesus was in one of the towns, a man came along who was covered with leprosy. When he saw Jesus, he fell with his face to the ground and begged him, "Lord, if you are willing, you can make me clean." Jesus reached out his hand and touched the man. "I am willing," he said. "Be clean!" And immediately the leprosy left him. *Luke 5:12–13*

Heal me, O LORD, and I will be healed; save me and I will be saved, for you are the one I praise. They keep saying to me, "Where is the word of the LORD? Let it now be fulfilled!" *Jeremiah 17:14–15*

JESUS, THE SERVANT

Whoever wants to become great among you must be your servant, and whoever wants to be first must be your slave—just as the Son of Man did not come to be served, but to serve, and to give his life as a ransom for many.   *Matthew 20:26–28*

Your attitude should be the same as that of Christ Jesus: Who, being in very nature God, did not consider equality with God something to be grasped, but made himself nothing, taking the very nature of a servant, being made in human likeness. And being found in appearance as a man, he humbled himself and became obedient to death—even death on a cross!
Philippians 2:5–8

The Sovereign LORD has given me an instructed tongue, to know the word that sustains the weary. He wakens me morning by morning, wakens my ear to listen like one being taught. The Sovereign LORD has opened my ears, and I have not been rebellious; I have not drawn back. I offered my back to those who beat me, my cheeks to those who pulled out my beard.... Because the Sovereign LORD helps me, I will not be disgraced.
Isaiah 50:4–7

I am the good shepherd; I know my sheep and my sheep know me—just as the Father knows me and I know the Father—and I lay down my life for the sheep.
John 10:14

GOD, THE JUST

Far be it from God to do evil, from the Almighty to do wrong. He repays a man for what he has done; he brings upon him what his conduct deserves. It is unthinkable that God would do wrong, that the almighty would pervert justice.
Job 34:10–12

God presented him (Jesus) as a sacrifice of atonement, through faith in his blood. He did this to demonstrate his justice, because in his forebearance he had left the sins committed beforehand unpunished— he did it to demonstrate his justice at the present time, so as to be just and the one who justifies the man who has faith in Jesus. *Romans 3:25–26*

Your throne, O God, will last for ever and ever; a sceptre of justice will be the sceptre of your kingdom. You love righteousness and hate wickedness.
Psalm 45:6–7

God is just: He will pay back trouble to those who trouble you and give relief to you who are troubled, and to us as well.
2 Thessalonians 1:6–7

The LORD is known by his justice.
Psalm 9:16

For the LORD is righteous, he loves justice; upright men will see his face.
Psalm 11:7

GOD, THE RIGHTEOUS

The LORD is righteous in all his ways and loving toward all he has made. The LORD is near to all who call on him, to all who call on him in truth. He fulfills the desires of those who fear him; he hears their cry and saves them. The LORD watches over all who love him, but all the wicked he will destroy.... Let every creature praise his holy name for ever and ever.
Psalm 145:17–21

I delight greatly in the LORD; my soul rejoices in my God. For he has clothed me with garments of salvation and arrayed me in a robe of righteousness, as a bridegroom adorns his head like a priest, and as a bride adorns herself with her jewels. For as the soil makes the sprout come up and a garden causes seeds to grow, so the Sovereign LORD will make righteousness and praise spring up before all nations.
Isaiah 61:10–11

The LORD is in his holy temple; the LORD is on his heavenly throne. He observes the sons of men; his eyes examine them. The LORD examines the righteous, but the wicked and those who love violence his soul hates. On the wicked he will rain fiery coals and burning sulfur; a scorching wind will be their lot. For the LORD is righteous, he loves justice; upright men will see his face. *Psalm 11:4–7*

I will always have hope; I will praise you more and more. My mouth will tell of your righteousness, of your salvation all

GOD, THE RIGHTEOUS

day long, though I know not its measure. I will come and proclaim your mighty acts, O Sovereign LORD; I will proclaim your righteousness. *Psalm 71:14–16*

GOD, MY GUIDE

Since you are my rock and my fortress, for the sake of your name lead and guide me. *Psalm 31:3*

I am the LORD your God, who teaches you what is best for you, who directs you in the way you should go. *Isaiah 48:17*

Teach me your way, O LORD; lead me in a straight path because of my oppressors ... I am still confident of this: I will see the goodness of the LORD in the land of the living. Wait for the LORD: be strong and take heart and wait for the LORD.
Psalm 27:11, 13–14

For this God is our God for ever and ever; he will be our guide even to the end. *Psalm 48:14*

Send forth your light and your truth, let them guide me; let them bring me to your holy mountain, to the place where you dwell. Then will I go to the altar of God, to God, my joy and my delight. I will praise you with the harp, O God, my God.
Psalm 43:3–4

Yet I am always with you; you hold me by my right hand. You guide me with your counsel, and afterward you will take me into glory. *Psalm 73:23–24*

I will lead the blind by ways they have not known, along unfamiliar paths I will guide them; I will turn the darkness into light before them and make the rough places smooth. *Isaiah 42:16*

GOD, THE SAVIOR

But now, this is what the LORD says—he who created you, O Jacob, he who formed you, O Israel: "Fear not, for I have redeemed you; I have called you by name; you are mine. When you pass through the waters, I will be with you; and when you pass through the rivers, they will not sweep over you. When you walk through the fire, you will not be burned; the flames will not set you ablaze. For I am the LORD, your God, the Holy One of Israel, your Savior. *Isaiah 43:1–3*

For God so loved the world that he gave his one and only Son, that whoever believes in him shall not perish but have eternal life. For God did not send his Son into the world to condemn the world, but to save the world through him.
John 3:16–17

My soul finds rest in God alone; my salvation comes from him. He alone is my rock and my salvation; he is my fortress, I will never be shaken. *Psalm 62:1–2*

The salvation of the righteous comes from the LORD; he is their stronghold in time of trouble. The LORD helps them and delivers them; he delivers from the wicked and saves them, because they take refuge in him. *Psalm 37:39–40*

Surely God is my salvation; I will trust and not be afraid. The LORD, the LORD, is my strength and my song; he has become my salvation. *Isaiah 12:2*

GOD, THE GOOD

The LORD is good, a refuge in times of trouble. He cares for those who trust in him. *Nahum 1:7*

Give thanks to the LORD, for he is good; his love endures forever. *Psalm 107:1*

Which of you fathers, if your son asks for a fish, will give him a snake instead? Or if he asks for an egg, will give him a scorpion? If you then, though you are evil, know how to give good gifts to your children, how much more will your Father in heaven give the Holy Spirit to those who ask him! *Luke 11:11–13*

Good and upright is the LORD; therefore he instructs sinners in his ways. He guides the humble in what is right and teaches them his way. All the ways of the LORD are loving and faithful for those who keep the demands of his covenant. *Psalm 25:8–10*

How great is your goodness, which you have stored up for those who fear you, which you bestow in the sight of men on those who take refuge in you. *Psalm 31:19*

Taste and see that the LORD is good; blessed is the man who takes refuge in him. *Psalm 34:8*

I will sacrifice a freewill offering to you; I will praise your name, O LORD, for it is good. For he has delivered me from all my troubles, and my eyes have looked in triumph on my foes. *Psalm 54:6–7*

JESUS, THE SON

The Father loves the Son and has placed everything in his hands. Whoever believes in the Son has eternal life, but whoever rejects the Son will not see life, for God's wrath remains on him. *John 3:35–36*

His Son, who as to his human nature was a descendant of David, and who through the Spirit of holiness was declared with power to be the Son of God by his resurrection from the dead: Jesus Christ our Lord. *Romans 1:3–4*

For just as the Father raises the dead and gives them life, even so the Son gives life to whom he is pleased to give it. Moreover, the Father judges no one, but has entrusted all judgment to the Son, that all may honor the Son just as they honor the Father. He who does not honor the Son does not honor the Father, who sent him. *John 5:21–23*

The Son is the radiance of God's glory and the exact representation of his being, sustaining all things by his powerful word. After he had provided purification for sins, he sat down at the right hand of the Majesty in heaven. *Hebrews 1:3*

Jesus answered ... "Anyone who has seen me has seen the Father ... I am in the Father and ... the Father is in me. The words I say to you are not just my own. Rather, it is the Father, living in me, who is doing his work. *John 14:9–11*

CHRIST, THE LORD

In the beginning was the Word, and the Word was with God, and the Word was God. He was with God in the beginning. Through him all things were made; without him nothing was made that has been made. In him was life, and that life was the light of men. The light shines in the darkness. *John 1:1−5*

In him we have redemption through his blood, the forgiveness of sins, in accordance with the riches of God's grace, that he lavished on us with all wisdom and understanding. And he made known to us the mystery of his will according to his good pleasure, which he purposed in Christ, to be put into effect when the times will have reached their fulfillment—to bring all things in heaven and on earth together under one head, even Christ.
Ephesians 1:7−10

For in Christ all the fullness of the Deity lives in bodily form. *Colossians 2:9*

He is the image of the invisible God, the firstborn over all creation. For by him all things were created: things in heaven and on earth, visible and invisible, whether thrones or powers or rulers or authorities; all things were created by him and for him. He is before all things, and in him all things hold together. And he is the head of the body, the church; he is the beginning and the firstborn from among the dead, so that in everything he might have the supremacy. *Colossians 1:15−18*

CHRIST, THE LORD

God exalted him to the highest place and gave him the name that is above every name, that at the name of Jesus every knee should bow . . . and every tongue confess that Jesus Christ is Lord.

Philippians 2:9–11

PERSONAL PRAISE PASSAGES

PERSONAL PRAISE PASSAGES

PERSONAL PRAISE PASSAGES

PERSONAL PRAISE PASSAGES